# Chop! Chop! Chaplain!

*Chaplain Ministry in a Beef Processing Plant*

*Rev. Heidi Revelo*

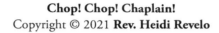

**Chop! Chop! Chaplain!**
Copyright © 2021 **Rev. Heidi Revelo**

Stratton Press Publishing
831 N Tatnall Street Suite M #188,
Wilmington, DE 19801
www.stratton-press.com
1-888-323-7009

ISBN (Paperback): 978-1-64895-456-6
ISBN (Ebook): 978-1-64895-457-3

Printed in the United States of America

# Contents

Chop! Chop! Chaplain! ...................................................5

Scarf Connection .........................................................8

Bless You, My Cow........................................................11

Saying Goodbye ..........................................................14

What's Worth Living For? ................................................17

The Right Words .........................................................20

When There Are No Words................................................22

Pedro....................................................................24

Paparazzi! Am I Famous?! ................................................26

What They Don't Teach You...............................................29

Celebrate!...............................................................33

Mecca Glow ..............................................................37

Going to Hell............................................................39

Laura....................................................................43

Fairy House .............................................................45

Almost Nothing, Almost Naked ...........................................48

Names...................................................................51

Pandemic Chaplaincy.....................................................54

One in Every Crowd .....................................................59

One Liners ..............................................................61

Lead a Horse to Water...................................................64

My God, Your God .......................................................67

# Chop! Chop! Chaplain!

T he beef-processing plant had an opening. The 2,800-employee facility (3,000 if you include subcontractors) wanted a part-time chaplain. The plant was 70 percent Hispanic (Mexico, Guatemala, Honduras, etc.), 20 percent African/African American (Somalia, Sudan, South Africa, Kenya, etc.) and 10 percent others (Asian countries, Philippines, "white").

They called for an interview. I arrived at the plant. I got out of the car, straightened my jacket, and tried to look like I wasn't nervous as I passed sixty feet of windows. I arrived at beautiful double glass doors at the end of a smooth walkway planted with ornamental trees and shrubs. I pushed the door. Nothing. I pulled the door. Nothing. I pushed and pulled the other door. Nothing. I waited a moment, sure someone would open it from the inside, say they were so sorry, and let me in. Nothing.

I looked inside like a kid smashing their face against the glass to see the prize inside. I saw the shiny tiled entryway, tall receptionist desk, and classy waiting room chairs.

I looked around, deciding what to do. The only people I saw were on the far side of the building, so I walked back down the walkway, followed the sidewalk past all of those windows, and there I found another door with two ramps and a set of stairs. People came in and out, so this door must be open. I passed people sitting against the building clad all in white like nurses, but with hard hats. They were smoking or talking on their phones and had little notice for me.

I got inside two sets of double glass doors. I was supposed to be looking for security. To the right was a line of closed doors. To the left were vending machines and chairs. I continued forward, and around the next corner was a rectangular room complete with a wall of windows five feet from the floor to the ceiling above a wall lined with counters and a guard. A uniformed security guard slid a glass door sideways like a drive-through burger joint. I signed in and was asked to wait in the lobby.

I returned to the vending machine room and found one of the preformed plastic cupped chairs screwed together unceremoniously on metal bars and legs. The floor was cement. The vending machines were the only color in this world of gray walls and gray floor. I waited.

A tall, thin, lanky black man sat close to me. While my 4'11" frame left my feet off the floor if I slid back in the chair, this man's arms and legs dangled like wet spaghetti as he slouched to one side with his eyes closed. I sat down, and he awoke. We made eye contact. I smiled and nodded. After a few minutes of silence, he spoke. "Do you work here?" English wasn't his first language, but I understood.

"No," I said, "but I want to."

"What job?" he asked.

"Chaplain," I answered.

His face tensed as his mind entered 'chaplain' into his brain's search box to dig through the bytes of information in his brain. His face lit up as he thought he found the answer. "Oh, chop-lain," he said, trying to repeat what I had just told him. He sat up, making a chopping gesture across his throat and neck. "You chop-chop the heads off the cows, right? A chop-lain?"

"No." I shook my head. How was I going to explain this? "It's like a pastor or counselor. We help people."

I thought that answer sounded lame, but I didn't know what else to say with the images of headless cows swirling around my thoughts.

He asked me more questions, and I learned a little about him before I was called to the interview.

As I was whisked off down another hallway, he said, "Good luck!", giving me a thumbs-up.

# Scarf Connection

"You *touch* them?" someone asked me. It sounded perverse and disgusting. My mind froze for a moment. Was this white person I'd known for years really asking me if I touched other people? They already knew I was a chaplain. They knew I wasn't deviant.

I quickly flashed through several snapshot moments of my daily dealings with people. Filling out applications. Talking to people in my office. Saying hi in the hallway. We'd wave and raise our voices above the noise.

"Hi!"

"Hi there!"

"How are you today?"

We'd talk one-on-one in the hallway, in a room that wasn't occupied, or in my postage stamp–sized office I shared with the other chaplain. Our hands touched when I handed them a pen. I'd hugged many women. I'd fist-bumped a few men, and some had offered their hand in a handshake.

I snapped back to the question at hand. "You *touch* them?"

I like to think the person asking the questions heard their own question as they said it, imagined a stenographer in a court room reading it back to them, and suddenly felt shame and guilt at the racism and lack of respect. I believe their mind ping-ponged to the next question before I answered.

I had no professional experience working with multiculturalism. No thesis. No long research study. No specialization of classes. No high-caliber reading lists and mind-warping immersion adventures. I had real-life experience, which I thought was fine. Of course, I knew this would be different from pastoring a church, but I believed I treated people as people—with respect and dignity. If I could see them as individuals, maybe they too could see me as an individual.

From the first job interview, it was apparent the chaplain would be expected to work with people of other languages, cultures, and traditions. I thought by applying for the job, I was communicating that I was willing to do this. They asked me anyway and seemed to pause, sit back, and peruse my expression, then look at me sideways when I answered. They seemed to be waiting for me to ask for clarification, specifics, or for me to spit out some magic answer. I didn't have one.

As I was introduced to people in the plant and in the community, there was a barrage of similar questions. Experience working with Africans and Hispanics? Had I done anything like this before? I had not been wary of this before, but now I wondered what terrible predicament I had put myself in. What did the rest of the town and plant know that I didn't? Suddenly, I was in a building with 2,800 people who were different than myself, and I was not only not ready, maybe I was doomed.

I stood in the hallway during shift change while half the people left and half arrived for the next shift. It was loud, fast, and crazy. A Somali lady came in through the front door and was headed off to processing when I saw her. She had on a burka, a traditional dress that covers a woman from top to bottom, down her arms to her fingertips, all the way to the floor, and her head was wrapped in a hijab. Not just a hijab; it was a vibrant blue, almost teal. It covered her head, over her forehead, and wrapped around her face. It fell over her shoulders and flowed halfway down her back. It was my favorite color, and the light made it dance and shine like a halo.

I moved toward her without thinking. I don't remember doing this. My hands reached for the edge of her hijab, and the silky fabric caressed my fingers. The woman stopped, looking startled, but I didn't notice. "Ohhhhh, I love your scarf," I cooed. I sounded like a third grader standing in front of Cinderella minutes before the ball. I stroked the scarf softly. "It's so beautiful," I said, looking up. I caught a glimpse of her startled expression before her face melted. She looked down, as if embarrassed, and then our eyes met. A smile started at the corner of her mouth and turned into a grin.

Now I was the one unnerved. What was I doing? I had better manners than this. I didn't just walk up to people and grab their clothing. I was so ashamed, but I was still holding the scarf. The look in her eyes forgave my forward approach. She heard the compliment and knew I wasn't pretending. This was real.

"Thank you," she whispered.

"Oh, I'm sorry. I'm so sorry," I said.

Her smile got bigger instead of smaller. With a quick dip of her head toward the floor, she turned and disappeared into the line of people headed for the stairs. We still smile at each other and say hi. There's no self-consciousness for either of us. We're friends. We made a connection!

# Bless You, My Cow

**W**here do you work?

I work at a beef processing plant.

Oh, wow. What do you do?

A list of possible job titles includes accounting, bone chuck, community liaison, employment, engineer, ergonomics, freezer, FSQA, gutter, harvest (it's no longer politically correct to say slaughter), hides, material handling, offal, packaging, processing, push beef, rendering, safety, sales, skirt puller, superintendent, supervisor, supply, yards…and on the list goes.

My answer is simply, "I'm a chaplain."

There's a pause where the world stops and counts to three. Some people know. "Oh, a chaplain. Is that like a pastor?" they ask.

"Yes, it's like a pastor or a counselor."

If an employee needs someone to talk to, they can talk to the chaplain. If they need help with an issue—anything from depression to children, relationships, finances, health, all the stresses of life— they can talk to a chaplain. Chaplaincy includes counseling, spiritual care, and social work.

Then comes the dreaded question.

"Do you pray for the cows?"

Yep, I've been asked over and over. No, I don't pray over the cows.

To be fair, it's not a completely unhinged question. Muslims must carry out the slaughter and say a prayer, known as the tasmiya or shahada, during the harvest process. The process of kosher slaughter for those of Jewish faith also involves praying a blessing over the harvest.

Again let me say it, *no*, I do not pray over the cows. The purpose of a chaplain is to assist people in their daily lives. If a person is happy at home, then they're happy at work. Maybe they need a little help. Let me give you a colorful explanation.

Oliver and Amelia have been dating for two years. They love each other very much. One day Oliver is working in processing, and he's having trouble concentrating. He makes a cut with his knife, and it slips. He recovers, cleans his knife, clears his head, and prepares for the next piece. He messes it up again. His supervisor can see he's struggling, so he tells the person to take a ten-minute break and talk to the chaplain.

Oliver arrives with a heavy heart. "Chaplain Heidi," says Oliver, "I love my girlfriend very much. Amelia and I are perfect together, but there's one problem." Oliver dabs at a tear and continues valiantly, even though he's nervous to say this out loud. "Amelia comes to my apartment to watch a movie, and when she takes her shoes off, I can't breathe! All the oxygen is sucked out of the room, and the smell is awful—even worse than rendering! I bought her new shoes, but she says they're too nice to wear every day. I don't want to offend her, but I have to fix this! What can I do?"

First, please remember that what Oliver tells me is confidential. I will not run over to Oliver's friends enjoying lunch in the cafeteria and say, "Hey, you know what Oliver told me? You'll never guess Amelia's deep, dark secret!"

Now, as a chaplain, I am required to report if an employee is going to hurt themselves, hurt someone else, do damage to the company, or if it's harassment.

Oliver and I can talk. We can strategize and come up with some possible solutions to his problem. I'm not talking about this with anyone else, not even Amelia. No supervisor. No family member. No best friend. It's confidential.

With every orientation class I share this crazy example. People need to be able to talk about many things: betrayal, cancer, finances, fire, grief, injury, loss, mental illness, PTSD, tornadoes, unexpected parenthood—and the list of possibilities never ends. It's all confidential, though, if it doesn't involve those four earlier categories.

My goal in orientation is to keep everyone smiling while understanding the deep conviction I have for their privacy. I could give a Hallmark Movie Channel example of some sad, despairing, despondent, desolate bloke at the end of hope. It would probably be memorable, but it would be a real downer.

Instead, the new employees giggle at the idea of a girlfriend with stinky feet. There's often a girlfriend/boyfriend sitting next to each other in orientation class, and they glance at each other, smirk, and look away.

Even smirks are confidential.

# Saying Goodbye

I was early enough. I wouldn't show up embarrassingly late. Somalian funerals are at the graveside, so I couldn't slip into a back pew if I was a few minutes late, and I certainly didn't want to drive up to a graveside service late.

I walked slowly toward the two Somalian men standing at the side of the grave. The two men scattered like rats and huddled together two hundred feet away, so I stood at the head of the grave and waited a moment.

The service was scheduled for 10-ish, which meant sometime around 10:00 a.m. It wasn't an exact time, and many cultures I work with experience time as fluid, moving, inexact. I was prepared to wait. It was Sunday morning of Labor Day weekend. I was missing my own church service.

The city employee approached. "I'm surprised they let you be here," he said. He told me the men came close to the grave, and the women stayed back, even stayed in their cars...even when they buried babies.

Oh, that's why the men fled like rats. All day at work, the same men talked to me, stood close, communicated, asked for help. Couldn't even one of them explain it to me?

I called my boss, and she was still sleeping. "Am I supposed to be here?" I asked.

"Of course, just stand in the back with the women like we usually do," she told me. This was my first. There was no usual in my current experience.

I looked around to find a location close, but not too close. I determined what I would consider back far enough and then picked a tree twice as far away.

The cars started to arrive. It looked more like a caravan headed for a concert. My experience at graveside services was a handful of cars sharing rides of a close-knit group of relatives. Thirty cars came down the east gravel path. Then another twenty-five. From the west gravel path came twenty, then twenty more. It didn't matter which direction or how many after that because I wasn't counting. This felt strange...like this was concert parking or stadium football parking.

The cars stopped. Doors opened and closed. Men moved toward the grave. The religious elders wore long straight-line robes and flat-topped round caps on their heads. The women came toward me. I nodded at them since I couldn't smile with my mask on. Before the women arrived, I was without a mask breathing in sweet country air. Several women thanked me for coming. Wrapped in burkas, the breeze rippled through each one and all of them with a swoosh of dancing color. The group looked like a package of M&Ms scattered across the plain.

The mother and sister of the man they were burying came to be with the women, hugging each other tightly.

We watched as the men formed a group and prayed over the body. The sister and mother sat, so most of the women sat on the ground of stubbly, uneven tufts of hardy grass that had survived the plain's heat, cold, and wind for years. The mother cried, then wailed a curt, crying yelp in anguish. The nesting women shushed her, wiping away her years. There was no crying at these funerals. One was to believe the dearly departed was already in a better place.

Beyond the grave was a backdrop of short golden cornstalks in neat, straight rows, the image of the rich plains and the full harvest, as if the seasons too bowed for this man who died, and rows beckoned a natural pathway to the immortal.

The body was placed in the grave. Their tradition calls for burial within twenty-four hours, no embalming, no casket, but a vault. The men placed the body in the vault. It was strange to see the religious leaders' heads bob up and down as they did their work in the grave bottom. At a signal, a beat-up blue truck parked nearby backed up to the grave dangling a heavy vault lid as if it was a fish on a fishing pole. The lid descended, was released, and now he was entombed.

The men went to work shoveling dirt. Other cultures sprinkle a handful of dirt ceremoniously over the grave, but here the men filled the grave bottom to top. We heard their words of direction to each other.

A woman walking toward us screamed and fell forward. Panic threatened to take over. The nesting ladies ran to her aid. One stood and called clearly for help. Three men from the funeral site came, and a man with medical experience started over, but was waved away quickly. The woman wasn't in mortal danger.

The grave was filled, and the first leader spoke in Arabic. The second spoke in Somali and repeated in English. "And someday, we too shall die," he finished, sweeping his hand toward the fresh grave. The freight train blew its whistle, and I saw the picture of the train transporting his soul to its new home in my mind.

The young man who died was twenty years old. The same age as my youngest child. This was a little too personal and close. Leaving death in a blanket of analogy was easier.

# What's Worth Living For?

Jason made bad choices. More than one or two bad choices, and the consequences were catching up with him. He didn't want to share details—and that was fine with me. His large, tall frame sat curled up on the folding chair, and he cried.

"Hey, Jason," I said as I approached him. There was nothing private about the place we were in, but there were only a few people around instead of a flash mob. I put my hand on his shoulder. He didn't react. He didn't look up. He remained curled on the chair. His work boots told the story of a hard worker who came day after day without exception. He didn't have his hard hat, hairnet, earplugs, or equipment with him. To me that was a good sign. Those who show up with everything and are this upset usually quit on the spot, turn in their gear, and walk out the door.

"What's going on?" I asked as I pulled up another folding chair next to him.

He cried harder, his broad hand cupped around his forehead. His elbows rested on his knees, and he looked down. He started to shake as he cried. "I can't..." he said, and he started to shake again.

I sat quietly and waited. He wiped tears from his red, blotchy eyes with strong, hard-as-nails hands. I waited patiently. Chaplains are called to sit with people in pain.

"Can I help you with something?" I asked.

He shook his head back and forth quickly, reticent to ask for help or even talk about what he was facing and feeling. "I don't want to live," he choked out. "I want to kill myself." He moaned. The deep creases in his wind- and sun-hardened face told the story of a man who spent lots of time outdoors, worked with his hands, and worked hard.

He didn't want to say what the specific problem was so I asked a few questions.

"Are you married?"

No.

"Do you have kids?"

No.

"Do you have family around here?"

No.

"Where do you live?"

He told me, and then he said, "My house..." He was crying harder now. "I want my house..."

A lady raised an eyebrow at me as we looked at each other. Another woman was trying to dial the phone, but her finger was paused over the keys, suspended while she watched this young man's trauma.

I was at a loss. Was he saying he wanted his house? Did he want to go home?

"Is anybody at your house right now? Do you have roommates?" I asked.

No. No roommates. He lived alone except for his horse.

"Oh, horse. I bet he's very special," I said, realizing he wasn't saying *house*, but saying *horse*.

Jason nodded his head up and down, the tears still falling. Jason didn't want to tell me about his horse—gender, color, name. "I want my horse," he repeated.

"Jason, you said you didn't want to live. Do you plan to hurt yourself?" I asked.

He didn't respond. I sat with him for another twenty minutes with a few questions, but mostly silence and support. "You can get through this. We can find a way," I told him. "Jason, you said you wanted to kill yourself. Can you promise me you won't hurt yourself?"

He wouldn't say yes. No family in the area. No wife or kids. Lived alone, no roommates. I didn't think it was a good idea for this person to go home.

Things were happening behind the scenes. I could tell decisions were being made. I excused myself and talked to an HR manager.

"Well, he threatened to hurt himself, so our next step is to call the police," they said.

The police were called. He agreed to go with them, and they quietly exited the building, got into the police car, and drove away.

Later I learned he convinced the police he was fine, and they took him home. I was hoping they'd find him a safe place to stay, a counselor to talk to. I was hoping he would receive a mental evaluation and resources instead of just a ride home.

He didn't take his life, and for that, I'm grateful every day. It's important to find even one thing a person can live for. In this case, it was his horse, his best friend and companion, his confidant, his bestie.

# The Right Words

On the walls of our plant hang posters of upcoming events, important dates and deadlines, and plant closings (like the Fourth of July). We are a three-language plant, as one HR director put it, so we print everything in English, Spanish, and Somali. I would look at the Somali text. I would imagine what it sounded like. English and Spanish have quite a few similarities. Education in English. *Educacion* in Spanish. *Americano. Hamburgesa. Cliente. Popular. Melon. Idea.* In Spanish, each letter has one sound. If you know the sound, you can pronounce most Spanish. I noticed the first word of various Somali postings started with *Waxaan*. Waxaan—I tried pronouncing it in my head the way I thought it would sound.

In the HR office one day, the subject of language comes up. A Somali woman asks me what languages I speak. I'm feeling a little feisty that day, and I say, "Oh, I know some Somali."

What? What are you talking about? The shock on their faces is priceless.

That's when I went back to my newly learned word: *Waxaan.*

I explain how I read the postings. "Waxaan," I say as if I'm reciting Hamlet.

They look at me and try to figure out what Somali word I'm trying to say.

"Yes," I continue to explain, "I know Somali. Waxaan. You know, wax on."

Their brains are starting to hurt. I can see their brain cells flipping from English to Somali and back again. What is that lady trying to say?

"I've read the posters. There's the word W-A-X-A-A-N," I spell out letter by letter. "Wax ON," I say again with Shakespearean declaration.

The Somali lady shakes her head back and forth, as if her brain is seeking a stronger Wi-Fi signal. By now others are joining the conversation.

"Wax on! Yes! Just like *Karate Kid*! Wax on. Wax off."

Now they're all smiling and laughing.

"Oh, Heidi," says the Somali woman just above a whisper, but smiling ear to ear and shaking her head slowly in disbelief. "Heidi, the *w* sounds like an *h* in Somali."

For a few minutes, we all spoke Somali! Wax on. Wax off. Wax on. Wax off.

# When There Are No Words

There is a community of Micronesians at our plant. They come from a string of small islands in the South Pacific—think Hawaii. They speak their own language and they like to live together. No, I mean t-o-g-e-t-h-e-r. Three or four generations can live in the same house, including aunts, uncles, in-laws, cousins, everybody. In fact, it's a strange idea for them to think they'd all divide up into small families and live in separate areas.

A young couple's child was born prematurely and died. A local pastor provided a graveside service and asked if I could also be present. Nothing about this was easy or simple. It was a small group of family who attended. A few adults held bags with silk flowers. They handed out the flowers to the children in attendance.

There was no vase, no container. The parents were grieving, and the adults were holding it together for the moment, but that was it. I asked the children if they'd like to put the flowers at the head of the grave. Next thing I knew, I was down on my knees, finding a place to secure the flower stems. Then I heard the words of the father.

"No, kids. You're supposed to scatter the flowers in the…" His voice broke. I imagined how beautiful blue mountain lilies, hibiscus in a riot of colors, and purple Queen-basslets would look. What a wonderful tribute to the child they lost with the colors and fragrances. I could see the baby's spirit on a raft of scents ascending to heaven.

# Pedro

**M**eet Pedro—Hispanic, well-built, single, early twenties, strong family support. Everyone who knew him liked him (and the whole town knew him).

Pedro would use my office to work on labels for his job. Before his shift started, he had to write dates and data on rolls of labels. It's much easier to do this if you can sit down and use a desk, and my office was close to the office of his company, a subcontractor of the meat plant. He worked B shift, so in the middle of the day, he'd show up to do his labels. We said hi. We started talking.

Pedro was in his twenties, but his soul was about twelve. He was without a life calling. He didn't want to change the world, but he was in the world, and he wasn't sure what his role was. He was fun to talk to and tease. He had an impish grin. He hung out with a couple other guys at work, his buddies.

When I say we started talking, you might think we discussed the meaning of life, cosmic origin, or pondered other great questions. He mostly answered questions with yes, no, or a maximum of three words. I just kept asking him questions—nothing too personal.

Life had been hard for everyone. Long hours. Few days off. Extra-long shifts. Just enough time for people to do their laundry and start a new week again. I talked to Pedro's B shift supervisor. "I want to have a birthday party for Pedro," I said. No, it wasn't his birthday. I didn't even know when his real birthday was, but it just felt right.

The B shift manager thought I was a little scooters. "You want to have a party for a guy, and it's not his birthday?"

"Yep," I said.

"We never turn down a party!" he told me with a high five!

I told the people he worked with and invited them to bring a small gift or card if they wanted.

Friday came, and I hung a poster on the wall" "Happy Birthday Pedro!" I had a cake with a race car on it, race car plates, and race car napkins. Everyone got big pieces of cake—those clocking out and those about to clock in. It was smiles and happiness!

Pedro didn't have words. He mumbled a thank-you. He had never had so many people talk to him, pat him on the back, wish him luck, and tell him how glad they were just to be around him. The cake was going fast, and I knew by the time B shift let out, it would be gone.

"Do you want the car on the cake?" I asked.

His eyes lit up. He smiled—a real smile. He carefully pulled the car out, the frosting-laden tires trying to keep it on the cake, wrapped it in napkins, and stored it away. Like I said, his soul was twelve, and I saw Pedro flash that twelve-year-old sincere smile!

Pedro quit coming to work. He'd show up a few days, then be gone. He eventually lost his job. On Christmas Eve 2019, he died in a car accident. He'll always be Pedro with the race car, the smile, and the heart of gold to me. He's on my list of people to track down when I get to heaven and hear his whole story—even the parts that were too tender to share in this world.

# Paparazzi! Am I Famous?!

**W**orking around a large number of people has a few drawbacks. It was April, and I slept eighteen hours a day for three days. I pulled myself out of bed and slogged to the clinic. "It's allergies," the doctor said with confidence, and I felt like he wanted to pat me on the head while he took $150. I wasn't doing anything—none of the things I liked to do and none of the important things like laundry and dishes. What was worse, I didn't really care if every dish and every stitch of clothing piled up in the corners of the house.

Another day. I groaned and rolled out of bed. I got dressed and went to work. "Please stay home if you are sick" were the ironic words buzzing through my mind as I remembered the PowerPoint video I had recently seen.

This begins the great conundrum of each of our lives. Am I sick enough to miss work? No, it's allergies! I'm not really sick at all.

As I shared my experience of swelling sinus cavities, dizzy red eyes, clogged ears, and a nonstop dripping nose, the everyday nonprofessional, nonmedical, and untrained people told me, "That's not allergies." Another professional checked me out. I paid him $150 as they offered up a sullen and sad look with great empathy, but no solution.

I was so tired. I was sick. I was sick and tired of being tired and sick. What else could I say? I opened the door to yet another clinic, now a week after the first allergy endorsement, and found one of those highly efficient attractive women who typed my information into a computer and hit Enter. I felt like death warmed over. I could sleep standing up as they entered more information and cross-checked its accuracy for what seemed like the twentieth time. Would this horrible feeling ever leave? I could curl up like a cat and sleep on this waiting room floor for all I cared.

I gave myself a pep talk. *You can do this, Heidi. You're almost there. You're just feet away from seeing a doctor. Hold on.* Finally I was in the magic system of all wholeness and medical care, and they would help me! Well, not quite.

"We don't have a provider for you," explained Ms. Efficient at her keyboard. "You'll have to go to Urgent Care."

I must have given her that look of "What are you talking about?"

She pointed across the street and directed, "Urgent Care."

In three more weeks, it was rumored Urgent Care and the clinic would perform a tango dance and unite under one organizational structure. But not yet.

I departed. My mother taught me to follow sidewalks and be polite, but I didn't care. I set off across the grass, determined to cross the road and find Urgent Care before it disappeared down another rabbit hole. I took two steps across the grass when it happened. A lady with a high voice and enough energy to light up a dozen solar panels came charging out of the clinic door. "Heidi! Heidi! Oh, *there* you are," she squealed as she ran up to me.

She didn't notice I was halfway to dead. She didn't see I was praying for enough energy to get to Urgent Care and sit down again. She didn't notice I was moving at a snail's pace, my eyes like hollowed-out walnut shells.

"I've been looking for you *so-o-o* long!" the woman gasped, happily jangling on and on. Her jewelry caught the sun and glinted. Her bracelets sang their own ditty. She didn't walk—she nearly hopped with enthusiasm. What on earth could this woman need from me?

"As you know," she said, although at the moment, I didn't know or remember anything, "I look at apartment." She was sure she'd found the answer to the greatest questions of her life. "I *need place*," she repeated, wrapping her burka-enshrouded left arm around me from the side. She dropped her arm quickly and spun to face me. "I *need* place," she insisted.

Is this what it's like to be stalked by the paparazzi? So many people dream of fame, but this is as close to paparazzi as I want to get. People chasing me around clinics, popping up, and asking questions. I think that was my two seconds of fame!

# What They Don't Teach You

"Chaplain Heidi, we'd like you to do a wellness check," they told me. This employee hadn't been to work in several days. His work history was spotty. He'd come for a day, then not show up. Repeat. He almost never made it on a Monday or Friday. He was supposed to call in and tell the company he wasn't coming and why. He was supposed to be talking to his supervisor. His supervisor was supposed to have the employee's personal phone number and vice versa. Sometimes policy and procedure didn't mirror reality. Go figure.

I arrived at the young man's address and knocked on the door. A woman answered. Yes, she knew Ricky. Ricky was her son. She introduced me to her husband, who was also Ricky's father. They explained that since their move from the West Coast, life had been very difficult for Ricky. He wasn't adjusting well, and they hoped I could help him. Mom and dad were both upset. They knew their son needed help. They had tried everything to help him find a healthy, happy life.

His grandmother lived down the road. Grandma had offered him a place to live—his own place. His own house, own space, a bachelor pad that any twenty-something would drool over. He rarely went there, but preferred to be with mom and dad.

I appreciated how much the parents cared about their son. They said he was here, in the house, but so far I hadn't seen him. We were in the living room talking. I had said hello to the dad in the kitchen, and Ricky wasn't in the kitchen either. Maybe he needed a few minutes to get presentable, especially since he worked B shift. It's difficult to rise and shine early when one works late into the night.

I was starting to wonder if I got my wires crossed. Mom and dad were running out of things to say. Conversation was lagging, so I asked, "Can I talk to him?"

"Of course," they said, darting looks at each other and holding stiff smiles on their faces. Something was going on, but what weren't they saying? They led me down the hall, knocked twice on a bedroom door, and slowly opened it. "Ricky, the chaplain from work is here to see you."

I couldn't see into the room as mom and dad stuck their heads in, obviously hoping for a sign of…something.

I put on my best smile and stepped forward as they waved me in. Chaplains have to be careful. It's best not to place one's self into a situation where someone can claim you did or said something inappropriate. I didn't like this setup. I had hoped Ricky would come into the living room to talk to me. It's better to be in open areas, and if he didn't want to talk in front of mom and dad, we could make arrangements of some kind.

I stepped through the door, and there was the mighty, muscular, prime-of-life young man facedown in bed! Here was a man old enough to vote, old enough to drink (finally), old enough to own a car, old enough to get married, old enough to climb mountains, forge rivers, chase rainbows, and all I could see was the back of his short haircut and a river of flowing rumpled white sheets.

I was in shock. A moment ago I was worried about entering a young man's bedroom and didn't want to see anything too personal, but now I was considering the best way to talk to the back of a skull.

We talked. His answers were mostly short grunts of yes and no. Previously he lived near a group of friends who gamed with headsets. They gamed and talked day and night. They were their own platoon, their own BFFs. When moving to Nebraska, he left all his friends, his support network, his gaming family, his battle buddies. Now he went to work to process meat and then home to…nothing. Of course, mom, dad, and grandma were there, but none of his friends. He hadn't made any new friends either.

His parents realized he was depressed. They knew it was traumatic for him to leave his friends. They also thought it was time a young son in his prime should be out making money, on the lifelong search for that "special someone," and setting bigger goals instead of racking up high scores on fantasy games with pretend outcomes. Now they didn't know what to do. Neither did I.

This young man and more than I'd care to count are mired in depression. Depression can't be explained. If your stomach hurts, you point to your tummy and say, "Pain. I have pain here." Depression is ambiguous. No desire to get out of bed. No desire to do anything. No joy in the events of life one is participating in. So of course, many stop participating in the short menu of activities of their life. Some say depression is being inside a hole with no way out. There's light at the top—or so everyone tells the depressed one. How does one reach that open space where joy, peace, and happiness abide? Everyone has a different answer: chocolate ice cream, running eight miles a day, counting Facebook likes, moving up the ladder of success, making money, adopting a dog, etc.

To those in the middle of depression, death looks like a sweet end to the awful turmoil going on inside, the inability to get up, the lack of motivation. Then our society adds on a layer of guilt. Then a layer of "pull yourself up." Then a layer of shame. Even Christian speakers and leaders talk this great game of changing your own life in three easy steps, a quick tug on your own bootstraps, a simple abra-cadabra. It's not that easy, and no two people experience it the same, except that it's awful for everyone.

I don't know what happened to this young man. He wanted to return to the West Coast, but he couldn't afford to go alone, and his parents were happy with their new jobs, the money they were mak-ing, being close to grandma.

He eventually lost his job because he stopped coming to work. I gave him and his parents all the resources I could find. I still pray for him, and I hope he's one I meet in heaven someday, and we get to talk. I hope his story goes something like "And that's when I met the love of my life…after three kids and two promotions…mentored young men…retired…whittled wooden spoons…taught grandson to fish."

# Celebrate!

The world waits for something great to happen. We grind away day in and day out, waiting for the moment of "it." The moment of achievement, meeting the goal, passing the mark, succeeding. Everyone waits.

I'm not a quiet chaplain. I'm not one who sits in the corner in quiet contemplation with a whisper of an answer once a millennium. I'm more of the "all hands on deck, give it to me straight, let's see how many people can have a better day today because we're all here" kind of lady.

Housing is tight in our town. Our town is the county seat. People arrive after news they've been granted an interview. They get hired. Life is great!

"Where can I get a bus schedule?" asks someone.

"Sorry, no buses here except school buses."

"Taxi?" they ask.

It's hard not to laugh. Taxis are in movies. There are no taxis in our town. The people arriving from large cities can't believe it. They think we're messing with them. To be honest, there is one bus. You call a phone number, they put you on the list for that day, and it costs $2 per ride. It's booked 10:00 a.m.–2:00 p.m., picking up senior citizens and transporting them to the Grand Generation Center for lunch, and from noon to 2:00 p.m., the bus takes everyone home. Oh, and they only work daytime hours. No early mornings for A shifters, and no late evenings for B shifters.

"How do you get around?" people ask.

We drive. Many coming from large cities or other countries have never learned to drive. There is no fourteen-year-old school permit for students who live outside the city limits in Mexico, Guatemala, or Somalia.

No bus schedule. No taxi.

We return to the original question of housing.

"I need a place to live," they say.

I pull out my list of landlords and circle a couple listings. "This is your best bet," I tell them. "You can call, or you can go to their office. They are very good at helping people and getting them in as soon as possible."

"We're looking for a two- or three-bedroom house close to the school with a fenced yard," they explain to me.

"Well, this list of landlords is primarily apartments and trailer houses, but you can ask," I say.

"Will they take dogs?"

No.

"Will they take cats?"

No.

"Is this close to the plant?"

No, not really.

In other locations, especially cities, it's not difficult to find a place to rent. They look at my list. When I started this position, I threatened to make a T-shirt and wear it around the plant that said, "I Do Not Have a House for Rent."

"We'd like a house with a fenced yard and a landlord that accepts small dogs," said more people than I can count. Hence the T-shirt: I do not have a house for rent.

"What about this one?" They point to a name on the list, the closest apartment complex to the plant.

"They have a six-month waiting list," I explain.

"No, no. People are moving out right now," they explain.

I can only nod. "Yes, people are moving out, but the people moving in are the ones at the top of the waitlist—which stays around six months."

"I have a section 8 voucher," explains another.

For families who need a four-bedroom unit, there's only two in town within the city housing program, and there's a longer wait, usually several years. There are low-income government-subsidied apartments, but only two children can be in each bedroom, and they have to both be girls or boys. The maximum is three bedrooms. If a family has too many boys or too many girls, their application is denied.

Many people don't seem to hear what I've said. I don't have a house for rent. I have been known to tell a few, "I could get you a tent, but it's October, and that's not a good idea." Then I smile. (Of course I wouldn't expect anyone to live in a tent.)

Now we're back to the apartment complex that's within walking distance of the plant. Everyone wants to live there. It's at least a six-month wait, a nineteen-page application, and so much red tape we could call it Huskerville. It happens though. For those who try, jump the hoops, fill in the blanks, provide all the information…they get an apartment!

"Woohoo!" I've been known to shout from my desk, both fists punching up in the air. "You got an apartment! We did it!"

The woman floats into the office in her swaying burka, smiles to the ceiling, fists in the air. "Yes! I got it! Thank you, Chaplain Heidi! Thank you!"

Those are the celebration moments. She hasn't signed the lease. She hasn't paid the rent, deposit, or electric deposit. She's been sleeping on her friend's couch for six months, and her kids have been sleeping on the floor, but today is the day we celebrate! It's finally come! She'll have an apartment all her own for herself and her kids. We're not holding out to celebrate for Ramadan, Christmas, or National Cupcake Day. We're celebrating today! She got an apartment!

# Mecca Glow

M eet Naji. He's one of my favorite people. He's Somalian, over six feet tall, and skinny as a string bean. I asked his secret to being tall. He said it was a gift from his mother and father, both tall, and years of drinking camel's milk. He speaks and writes many languages, including Arabic. He has private tutoring lessons with his daughter to teach her to write and read Arabic. He has a busload of kids, a full-time job at the plant, operates an African store, and is a spiritual leader in the mosque. *And*...he went to Mecca.

Mecca (or Makkah) is a city in western Saudi Arabia considered by Muslims to be the holiest city of Islam and its spiritual center. The prophet Muhammad was born there, and it's where he taught. The pillars of Islam state that all Muslims with the means must undertake Hajj, a pilgrimage to Mecca, once in their lifetime.

Naji came around the corner of the glassed-in hallway of security. He opened the sliding window (like the one at your fast-food drive-through) and stuck his head through the window. "Heidi, did you know I went to Mecca?" he asked. He was glowing. He was almost giddy. If he was ten years old and had a birthday party with a pony, he couldn't have been happier. His eyes sparkled. He exuded a magnetic energy. He couldn't stop smiling that broad, beaming grin.

I want all people of faith to have that kind of glow, gleam, incandescence, shine. I want us to look so magnificently spectacular, nobody can pass us without saying or thinking, "Wow! I wonder…"

That's the way I see the best evangelism. People are so moved by the living faith inside us that they can't help ask questions, inquire, and seek out. Then we offer nuggets of inspiration and knowledge—not of ourselves, but of our faith, and the relationship builds.

> When Moses came down from Mount Sinai with the two tablets of the covenant law in his hands, he was not aware that his face was radiant because he had spoken with the LORD. When Aaron and all the Israelites saw Moses, his face was radiant, and they were afraid to come near him. But Moses called to them; so Aaron and all the leaders of the community came back to him, and he spoke to them. Afterward all the Israelites came near him, and he gave them all the commands the LORD had given him on Mount Sinai.
> When Moses finished speaking to them, he put a veil over his face. But whenever he entered the LORD's presence to speak with him, he removed the veil until he came out. And when he came out and told the Israelites what he had been commanded, they saw that his face was radiant.
>
> (Exod. 34:29–34, NIV)

# Going to Hell

I exited Security (where the chaplains' office is located) and immediately came face-to-face with Annie, who had come from the nearby orientation class and now stood behind a partition that protected her from through traffic. She was looking for me. Annie wanted to make sure she was talking to the chaplain. Annie, a white woman in her twenties, was reserved, quiet, but firm as she spoke. Her body language indicated she was ready for a fight or an argument, but hoped it wouldn't go that far.

"Are you the chaplain?" asked Annie. The straight shoulders of her light frame indicated this was serious.

"Yes," I answered, coming close to the counter that separated us. I didn't want people walking through our conversation.

She stared for a moment, as if not sure what to say. This is a common occurrence. I have learned to be patient and wait. People need time to process what they want to say and how to say it.

"I'm a Wicken," she declared. She watched for my reaction.

*Did she say Wicken?* I thought to myself. *Am I thinking of the same thing? Wicken. Witches. Spells. Incantations.*

My processing brain was interrupted as she blurted out, "Every chaplain I've ever met has told me I'm going to hell."

The feeling of astonishment hit me, then immediately rolled over into a ball of empathy for what she'd been through, anguish that any chaplain would say that, and a strong desire to protect and care for her. "What did you need?" I finally choked out. I could have started shaking and frothing at the mouth from being that close to evil, right? (I'm kidding.) I could have agreed with all the chaplains before me that yes, I concurred, she was going to hell. I could have asked what in the world she was thinking getting caught up in something like Wicken. I didn't. I saw a person in front of me, and I respected her beliefs. I didn't see the religion. I didn't see the cultural stereotypes. I saw the person in front of me.

I was met with another long pause. I waited patiently. I didn't act like I was in a hurry. I didn't want her to think I didn't take her seriously. I just waited. After a moment, I asked again, "What can I help you with?"

Annie had an answer. This was the part she'd practiced in her head, I'm guessing. "I'm Wicken. That's like a witch. I will need some time off from work to pray. On Halloween night, we pray at 10:00 p.m., and the most important is at midnight."

Annie worked B shift and got off work about 11:00 p.m., although there was no guarantee, and this wasn't the kind of job one clocked in at 8:00 a.m. and clocked out at 5:00 p.m. on the dot.

"That's exciting!" I said. I smiled big. My heart rate increased. I really was excited. I could already see us in HR asking for religious accommodation. That's what it's called. The Muslims working in the plant have religious accommodation to pray. There are five daily prayer times, and when those periods fall during regular work hours, they are allowed to pray. They may leave the floor, go to the Prayer Room, and pray. When they return, another Muslim person goes. The plant can't survive if all persons leave the floor and pray at the same time. There is also religious accommodation for members of the Church of Jesus Christ of Latter-Day Saints when our plant works on Saturdays because that's their day of worship.

I had taken on semiconspiratorial body language. I was ready to defend her right to practice her faith. I read her body language, and my reaction surprised her completely.

She froze, then her shoulders slumped, a startled look invading her once-careful gaze. Her near-defiant stance was draining out of her as we headed to HR.

Why did I take this approach? Every day I hear people voice their opinions of unfair religious accommodations. I also hear management say, "If you do it for one, you have to do it for all." Equality and fairness are our building blocks. I wanted to see if management attempted a double standard. Yes, I recognized this hit a hot button for me.

The HR manager was behind closed doors. No other managers were available. After checking with the HR clerks and looking over my options, we made a plan. "I'll continue to look into this for you until we get an answer," I assured Annie.

She returned to orientation, and I waited to be able to present what might be my closest opportunity to a television *Law and Order* case in front of a great, exalted, all-powerful human resources manager!

I went back to the drawing board. I did some online research. I learned more about Wicken, and I looked up the regulations about religious accommodation. In the end, it wasn't nearly as dramatic as any *Law and Order* episode. Because B shift ended before midnight, no accommodation would be necessary.

Again Annie came to find me and asked, "Did you find anything out about what we talked about?"

"Yes. Since B shift gets off before your prayer time, there will be no conflict. You should be fine," I explained.

"Oh really? So I should be off by then?"

"Yes. B shift varies a little, but I've talked to HR managers and orientation trainers, and they all say B shift lets out before midnight. However, if you foresee a problem, please let me know, and I'll help you in any way I can," I offered.

41

I was honored a person from a belief system often seen as "against" or "opposite" asked for assistance. The advocate in me rose to this challenge with happiness. In this location, so many factions are divided into groups, the "for" and "against." I could advocate for an individual's rights while upholding a larger umbrella of caring.

I was shocked other chaplains would blatantly tell anybody they were "going to hell." That's what she said. It shone light on the hypocrisy of chaplains. As a chaplain, I'm not supposed to be beating people up. I'm supposed to be supportive, caring, nurturing. Nobody ever found Jesus while someone was screaming at them, "You're going to hell!" It never made anyone pause in midstep, turn, and say, "Really? I never heard that before. Tell me more about hell and why I don't want to be there." They'd probably say, "If this is the way your Jesus treats people, I don't want to be with you and him in heaven, you loser."

I didn't bring up Jesus or Christianity. I struggle whether I should have gone that route, but every time I play it back, I don't see it working well because I would have been forcing my views into the conversation. It was a rare occurrence.

I saw Annie in the hallway, and she said, "Thank you for following up and finding an answer." She was a bit incredulous that she didn't get any negative feedback from HR, chaplains, or anyone at the plant. She smiled and thanked me. Her smile said it all. She was smiling ear to ear as she headed down the hallway like she was in second grade on her way to recess—just short of skipping.

I saw her several times, and she smiled and waved.

The sad addendum to this story is that her line got out late, and she missed the prayer time. She told me the other believers understood, but she was disappointed. There was one more spiritually significant date she wanted to participate in, and it started at 10:00 p.m. HR said she could leave early and communicated that with her supervisor. Her supervisor, when the moment came, refused to let her go.

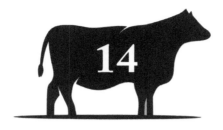

# Laura

I saw Laura often. We crossed paths, so to speak, frequently. She was always busy doing, planning, calling, emailing, texting, meeting, explaining, organizing, catching up, cleaning up, asking, insisting, pleading, explaining, mailing, copying, faxing.

I don't remember how it happened that the two of us talked. She asked me about my weekend and my family. I asked her the same. We talked for about ten minutes, and she suddenly changed. She'd been leaning back in a chair relaxed, arms crossed lightly, laughing as she told a story.

Her happy-go-lucky laugh changed to a wily smile. She looked at me sideways for half a moment before she snapped to attention. She sat up straight in her chair, both feet planted on the ground. She grabbed a folder, flipped it open, and acted like she was reading. She picked up her phone. That was my cue to leave.

I saw the real Laura! Do you understand how significant that is?! Some boast they shook hands with a president, got an autograph from a sports figure, shared a cab with a famous musician. I saw the *real Laura* for all of a few minutes before she looked at me like I had stolen the codes she keeps locked away to fire off nuclear weapons. (That's an analogy, folks.) Laura is private. She's in control at all times.

I saw the real Laura. I saw the side she almost never lets anyone see. It wasn't a secret, and there are no clandestine details to use in a tell-all documentary film. Laura, though, keeps her walls up. She plays her cards close to the vest. There's a time and a place to talk about personal things—when Laura decides it's appropriate, and that's never.

This is part of what chaplains do. We're not trying to be sinister. We're not out to uncover international secrets, interdepartmental collusion, gather intelligence on all the leaders' favorite ice cream flavors and weaknesses. We talk to people to develop relationships, to get to know them so that if and when the time comes they need someone to talk to…we have a foundation we've started building days, weeks, months, years ago, and it makes all the difference.

It doesn't matter to me if someone is a dog person or a cat person, but it's nice to know. It's nice to know who the Broncos fans are. It's interesting to know the guy who grows his own kale and makes his special-blend smoothies every day of the summer. It's nice to know the guy who has a heart for missionaries. Why? Because that's what makes an individual—their likes and dislikes, their passions and personalities.

# Fairy House

**M**aria had talked to me more than once. She loved her husband. She understood he had mental issues related to his life experiences. He drank too much. He was on disability, so financially he survived, paid the bills, and to the outside, he probably looked stable, but unhappy. Maria knew better.

He wasn't taking care of his child. He didn't have any time, energy, or effort. Their relationship was deteriorating.

"If I was him," said Maria, "I'd be working my program." If his life was a bicycle, he'd be spinning, but there'd be no traction. He was meeting with a few of the professionals he was supposed to be getting help from, but he was good at lying and making it sound good.

"When is it enough?" Maria asked me one day in tears. "I love him…but I don't know when it's time to…" Her voice faded off.

There was an awkward pause. I so wanted to jump in and say, "Oh, maybe he just needs time." The other part of me wanted to say, "Now! Get away from him now!" Chaplains shouldn't tell people when it's time to make decisions like these. It's their personal journey. The chaplain is there to listen, reflect back, to offer hope, and give a range of suggestions. This was another chaplain first for me. Essentially, she was asking, "Can I divorce him now?"

I wanted to take away her pain. I wanted her to feel free. I so wanted to say, "Go ahead, end it." I wanted to take away the uncomfortable living experience of not knowing what was coming day after day. Chaplains often don't get to say what they feel or want. They are called to assist.

"I can't tell you when it's time," I said to Maria. One side of my brain was considering the option of telling her how she'd know it was time.

1. When it's more than you can handle.
2. When he's not following his program.
3. When he wouldn't help himself anymore.
4. Give him a deadline to change and stick to it.

I knew the answer she really needed to hear though. "Whenever that time is, or if that time comes…I'll be here," I told her. There's no algebraic formula for these things. Every circumstance can change with a snap of the fingers. In the end, it was her decision, and I could see how much energy it was taking from her. I could also see another challenge she was facing: guilt.

"I'll also be here to take away any guilt," I said. For a moment, I was an illusionist performing a magic trick, and I waved my hands in the air, grabbing the guilt as if I was catching stars and securing the guilt. She could be free of the guilt, at least for a moment.

A few days later, I was in a store, and there were fairy houses—a new gardening trend. The idea was to build a little fairy garden in a potted plant or outside in your garden. There were houses, decorations, fountains. Imagine if Barbie moved into your houseplant pot, but Barbie was only three inches high, and Barbie had a green thumb. Barbie preferred being one with nature. Fairy wings replaced the Camaro. Toadstools replaced swag chairs. Barbie social events were now held in lush, green, rich-foliaged locations with tropical flowers. I chose a fairy house that was a cross between a tiny house and a dozen flowers tied into a bouquet. It was brightly colored and the size of a baseball. Perfect.

I went to see Maria. I was hoping to catch her alone, but that almost never happened. Chaplains have to keep confidentiality, of course.

"Hey, Maria, I have something for you." I pulled out the tiny fairy house.

"Ohhh, that's so cute!" said Maria.

The people around us weren't paying attention. Quickly I flipped over the plastic flowered house and flashed the bottom at her. "Guilt Receptacle" it read.

She paused a moment to read it. Then she smiled. "Oh, thank you," she said. Now she had a place to put all that guilt, nobody else needed to know about it, and it was cute to boot!

Healing is a process, you know. I can't say I've ever healed anyone. I see myself as a person who brings people closer to God, who offers some healing balm along the way. Our world lives in time, and time is represented by a line. Somewhere on the great line of time in our healing, Jesus sends people with medicine. Maybe it's Scripture, a nugget of an idea, a suggestion to help get us back on the straight and narrow path when we've wandered off, a new perspective.

*It's powerful. These moments of chaplaincy are what keep me going. I can see God using me. I don't have to see the end result. I don't have to know all the details. I know just enough to keep praying, and they trust me enough to come back if they need to or want to.*

# Almost Nothing, Almost Naked

Our beef-processing plant can only be successful with a large workforce. It's a collection of people, and some of the differences have left me wondering. Some women show almost no skin, and others I swear are almost naked.

Muslim women must be covered from the top of their head to their feet. You never see their hair. Sleeves come to their wrists. In even more conservative groups, women are required to wear a veil, and one can only see their eyes. It's a practice of purity and honor. Muslim women have two actions in response to fashion, color, and style: shoes and scarves.

The women wear gorgeous scarves of every fabric. Some have gold threads woven through them. The colors are more radiant than any rainbow or acrylic paint palette. They are silky, soft, patterned, solid, intricate, and show off each woman's personality.

Now "turn the page," and let me introduce you to the women modeling skinny jeans, leggings, crop tops, tank tops, beautiful leather boots (the cute kind, not the work kind), with fabric stretched every which way over their supple frames. Now add a splash of makeup.

Okay, some have a splash, and some dive headlong into lipstick, gloss, eye shadow, and mascara. There are piercings in any place you can find cartilage to hang something (you can Google that search on your own).

Now enter with me into the lobby of the plant. The cable of people snakes through two sets of doors, around security, through the lobby, up the stairs, and down the opposite side of stairs. Daily I run headlong into opposites. Some choose to cover their assets, while others do all but announce their arrival with flashing sequins, gemstones, faux fur, fishnet, and glitter.

To be fair, those cute boots, all piercings, and jewelry have to remain in a person's locker while they work. Before they swipe in and after they swipe out though, hold on to your hats, boys!

Yet everyone gets along. I've presented this as group 1 vs. group 2. They see each other as friends, coworkers on the line. To be able to work 260 days a year, share a locker room, eat in the same cafeteria, see people wearing garb their culture never even dreamed about…that takes maturity.

Overall, men have it easy. From any culture, their differences are much milder. Many African men like to look top shelf, sharp. They often arrive in buttoned-down shirts and peacoats (shall we say suit jacket, dinner jacket). They make sure it's ironed too, and I wonder if they're coming to work, or there's a gala ball I didn't know about.

Hispanic men have their own swag. Many like the cowboy hat and cowboy boots, whether they have a Tex-Mex background or not. They're ready for anything that comes their way. Young Hispanic males want a clean shirt, but they obsess more about their thick, sculpted hair; with just enough product, they hope it looks natural.

Understand there are people at every point on a wide continuum. Just like your community, our people are surviving work, home, kids, and life, so worrying about their cute outfit becomes less important as the responsibilities of life increase.

There are those I can laugh at though…or laugh with. An early twenties Somalian man, 5'8" (5'9" if you measured his hair), thin as a rail, entered the plant rocking a black T-shirt with Astrobright letters that spelled "Pep Club." Not many men can do that and carry it off, but he did (and he does). It's one of his favorite shirts.

A Hispanic man in his sixties comes to work dressed in layers. He wants to stay warm, and his favorite sweatshirt fits him perfectly. He just likes it. It's Astroturf green with a football sewn on the front punctuated by the words "Football Mom." Yes, he knows what it says. He likes the way it feels, and it keeps him warm. Good for him—sticking to his individuality.

# Names

**W**orking in a cross-cultural setting means I meet people with all kinds of names. Back in school, I knew four guys named Jeff and four girls named Amy, but this is an entirely different kind of paradox!

Barni is a Somalian human resources manager: professional, knows her stuff, proficient computer skills (that's no small task in the HR industry), and adept negotiator. That's right, Barni is a woman.

Sitting two desks from Barni when I started at the plant was a wonderful lady. She would help me with any of my crazy questions or needs. She was always looking something up for me so I could contact an employee. Her name was Nimo. To this day, I hear the name Nimo, and I see an artful swishing orange fish swimming to music. Then I have to swipe my brain left to the next listing of Nimo, and I now know multiple women named Nimo.

A new community liaison was hired. She was Asian from the Karen tribe. That looks like the woman's name Karen to you and I, but it's pronounced *Caw WREN*. She emigrated from Myanmar, formerly Burma, but she's not Burmese. The Burmese soldiers were not kind to the refugees, and to call the refugees Burmese is an insult. Her name was Ywe. Go ahead, you've now seen it in writing. How would you say it? She pronounced it *YOU' aye*. UA in HR terms is "urinary analysis." I whispered that to her one day, and I told her I just couldn't call her that! I called her *YAH way*, which is also the Old Testament word for God (YHWH), and she is a Christian.

Her husband's name is Sharmoo (*shahr MOO*). I couldn't figure out why that name sounded familiar, and then one day it hit me across the forehead. I create PowerPoint slideshows for our plant lobby, and I included a picture of Sharmoo alongside the famous Shamu, killer orca whale famous for shows at SeaWorld.

We have a person named Mustafa. Mustafa is one of the names of Muhammad, and it means "chosen, selected, appointed, or preferred." When I hear Mustafa, I see the waiter in *Ratatouille*, or I picture *Lion King*, but his name was Mufasa if you want to get technical. Again, I quickly have to swipe my brain left. It gets easier with time and repetition.

There are many male persons named Mohammed, and there are just about as many ways to spell it. I respect their name, but I had trouble keeping some straight. I earned a reputation for helping people process applications for a particular apartment complex. Once a few people worked through the application, passed the waiting list time, and moved into an apartment, they started telling others, "Go see that lady, the short one, Chaplain Heidi. She can help you, and we can be neighbors!"

At one point in history, I had three persons named Mohammed A. Mohammed. I had to keep them separate. How would I remember one from the other? I memorized their wives' names! As each one came in, I'd say, "Romisa is your wife, right?" (or their particular wife's name). As the third Mohammed A. Mohammed received the letter it was his turn to lease up, he came to affirm he was really moving in. "You always remember my wife! Not me!" he said. I had offended him, and I didn't realize it. He didn't understand that I was keeping my records straight!

There are times when some names make you shake with laughter. It's not the person's fault. You try like anything not to laugh, not to giggle, to keep a straight face. I never met this person, but his name was Say Moo. Go ahead, say it a few times, and see if you can introduce yourself with a straight face. It's harder than you think. It's a problem of languages. Their language has a lot of sounds like *poo, pee, wah, wee, ong, ing*. They're probably trying not to laugh at my name!

I hadn't worked at the plant very long, and I was learning names. I had a typed list in front of me. I openly sighed in relief. Here's a name I knew and could pronounce! I looked forward to meeting the young woman. My daughter had friends named Allie, Alli, and Ally. Then the person showed up—a young man whose name was Ali, as in Prince Ali. Another learning curve!

I am now working with six women:

1.  Fatuma S., baby due in August
2.  Fatuma A., baby due in August
3.  Fatuma H.
4.  Fatoma
5.  Fadumo
6.  Fartun

I think I need a new strategy!

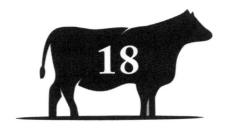

# Pandemic Chaplaincy

The previous stories happened before the COVID-19 pandemic, which, as I write, we are still experiencing. It changed us and our world.

Our beef plant stayed open because the president deemed us essential. While the schools, hair salons, businesses, restaurants, and government buildings all closed, I was still going to work and had a "regular" schedule.

Our plant created a temperature tent. Everyone enters through this door. Everyone wears a mask from the moment they put one foot on the property. There are hands-free hand sanitizer stations. Plexiglass is everywhere: around desks, made into individual cubicles in the cafeteria, meeting tables, etc.

People are dealing with some very basic issues no matter what their culture and language. Fear. What is coming? What happens if…when…what about…

The walls are plastered with posters in multiple languages with teaching graphics. The correct and effective way to wear a mask. A list of C-19 symptoms. How to avoid spreading the virus—coughing, using a tissue, etc. Directives for persons if they don't feel well or if they return to the plant after visiting a "hot spot."

As the first cases of COVID-19 were confirmed in our employees, the management said, "Chaplains, go visit them in the hospital." Wait. Hold your horses. Nobody is allowed in hospitals, not even family of the patient. Oh, whoops.

As chaplains, we discoursed about hope, and I told people, "Someday you'll tell your grandkids you lived during the COVID-19 pandemic, just like your grandparents told you about WWI, WWII, the Great Depression, or the Blizzard of 1888." They would smile just a bit, imagining that conversation with future generations.

There were all kinds of mythical remedies. Some people wanted to bathe in hand sanitizer. Some were claustrophobic, even though they came to work. They weren't used to spending every off-work minute at home. Others didn't want to leave their front door. I spent as much time debunking myths and playing down scaremongering as I did encouraging people. I liked to encourage people who believed a gallon of orange juice a day would cure C-19 to consider other possibilities and not cause damage to themselves in an attempt to stay well. Then I'd offer a hopeful thought to ponder the rest of the day.

We saw increases in suicidal thoughts, spouse abuse, depression, anxiety, addiction. Financial stress was evident. Parents had children at home. Some parents had child care, others did not. The normal child-care options were all shut down.

The beginning of May, I had a feeling. I can't explain except I felt I shouldn't be at the plant. With my preexisting medical condition and no company health insurance or disability pay if I did get sick because of my part-time status, it seemed prudent to stay home and stay well. While I was gone, three HR managers, one HR supervisor, the employment manager, and a plethora of people tested positive, and I spend a lot of time in those offices when I'm at work. I had asked if I could work from home, which I did for four weeks.

During that time, I sent cards to those out of the plant because of COVID-19. I mailed over four hundred cards to home addresses. I included notes in three languages. I also sent a how-to sheet to apply for a corporate program that would help persons financially up to $1,500, and now they could do it online in multiple languages.

I love greeting cards. A card comes in the mail. It's not a *ding* on the phone. It doesn't arrive on your desk, in your locker, under your windshield wiper (although it *can* arrive that way). There's something special about getting fun in the mail. What a wonderful diversion from whatever is weighing on one's shoulders. The daily pickup of the USPS mail followed by a quick sort of junk mail into file 13, and now the rest is bills and maybe a coupon you'll never use.

For many people, the card in the mail touches on a memory of birthdays long ago, birthday cards from Grandma and Grandpa, aunts and uncles. Their special day when getting older was an accomplishment, a rite of passage, and a joy.

A card is physical. In today's digital world, a card can be touched, held, opened, reread. I had a friend who put cards behind her light switches. Every room had a card slid behind the switch cover. When she entered and left rooms, the memory of the person sending the card, the message, and the joy of being remembered and cared about remained with her. I'm sure you're too young for this (ahem, let me clear my throat), but *in the olden days*, people kept a box of special memories—including cards. When life got hard, they went back to that shoe box, jewelry box, sock drawer, Trapper Keeper (oh, that is really, really old). If they need to take a walk through those memories—and encouraging words—one day or every day, they can.

"I just don't know what to write in a card" is the excuse I've heard. The message isn't important. Just sending the card means you are sending the message you're thinking about the person, that you care and want them to know you're in their corner, you're on their side, you're praying for them, you're not judging them, you're here for them even if it's thousands of miles away.

Send a funny card. Anytime you can get someone to laugh, it releases endorphins in their system, and those feel *good*. A supervisor couldn't locate someone on their line. The supervisor called. I called. The supervisor texted. I texted. Nothing. I went to their house and knocked on the door. Nobody answered. I left a birthday card at the front door even though I didn't know if it was his birthday. Guess what?! He called his supervisor!

I also try to send cards to people when I hear compliments about them. I heard management compliment a supervisor in a meeting. "He is doing a great job as supervisor. He talks to his people every day. He really cares about them." How come as people, we are quick to compliment people for their work, but not actually tell the person we're bragging about? I sent a card to the supervisor. (It's not easy to catch supervisors. Often a card is easier than tracking them down.) I went to the production floor, and he came to talk to me on the catwalk. I had to take out an earplug to hear him. "You sent me that card, right?" he hollered over the noise of the line.

"Yes." I nodded.

"Why?" he asked.

"Yes, I sent it," I repeated, hoping I was hearing him correctly.

"Why? Why did you send me that card?" he asked again, acting apprehensive. He spread out his hands like he was going to toss pizza dough as he repeated, "Why?"

"Oh, because you did such a good job. You're a very good super-visor. The company wants more people like you," I answered.

"That's it? I don't have to do anything?" he asked.

"Nope. No action required. Thank you for all you do."

His production line with his team of people took his attention away as he considered this, shaking his head back and forth as he moved toward the line. A card telling him he did well, and he didn't have to report, detail, return, explain, or file something in return? Wow.

What a great idea! What if my group did a mass mailing! Stop right there, buckwheat! All of us have the same reaction to mass mailings. When I get Burger King coupons in the mail, I put them in my pocket to use later, but I know it's not a personal, unique mailing just for me. Large organizations send out mass mailings, but can't figure out why people don't react with jumping jacks and flips. There's no personal touch. It's just another play for attention, another bribe to buy loyalty. Relationships are built, not bought.

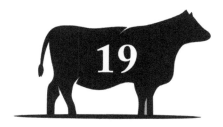

# One in Every Crowd

I met a man from Africa named George. He was probably in his fifties, but I'm only guessing. He was a smooth talker. It seemed there was always something he needed. There's one in every crowd—one person who needs extra help, extra time, extra assistance. That was George, and he wasn't shy about asking for help (or telling you he needed more than you were offering or had time for).

You know the kind of person I'm talking about, right? They've come to see you every day for months at a time. They sit in the chair by your desk like they're at home in their living room. We knew George was a handful. We knew he liked attention. We helped often, directed him to community resources, assisted him in finding help.

Mental illness is difficult to help people with. As a mentor told me, "Adults have the right to live under a bridge in a cardboard box if they want to and aren't breaking the law." When is someone mentally ill? How does a chaplain help them get an assessment if they are in denial? What if they aren't mentally ill, and it's only a chaplain's opinion? Pushing too far can step on their rights.

One day it happened.

"You know, we're still waiting for those pink tractors," he said.

"Did you say pink tractors?"

"Yeah, they never sent them. We're still waiting."

"Who is doing that, George?"

"The government. Yep, still waiting for them." He didn't say how many. He didn't explain any of the details, and we didn't ask. We knew George was a few crayons short of a full box, but we didn't have any idea he was looking for pink tractors! On the positive side, he has been evaluated, and he continues to live life without incident. He changes jobs and changes locations, but that's not a mental illness. He pays his bills and takes care of himself. There are no easy answers, but there's one in every crowd.

# One Liners

A trucker dropped off his trailer at the plant and left. His dispatch called to tell him his next load was ready. He showed up at the truck gate. "What am I hauling?" he asked security.

"Hides," they told him.

"How many chicken hides are in a load?" he asked.

You're at a *beef* plant, buddy, not a chicken plant."

(And besides, I like to eat my chicken hide extra crispy!)

\* \* \*

Two female persons are walking toward the parking lot. One is Hispanic. The other is African. "No no no," said the African woman to the Hispanic woman. "Not *hola*, Allah." (Read it out loud, it's funnier.)

\* \* \*

Ramadan was coming to an end. Ramadan is a month-long Muslim celebration of worship, prayer, and fasting. From sunup to sundown, they fasted. Many of our employees got up early and ate, then had to wait until sunset to eat again. If I was fasting, I wouldn't want to spend my break time in the cafeteria, and the locker room holds little entertainment, so many enjoy the fresh air outside. Those who work B shift can eat after sundown, but the thought of pulling out leftovers to reheat wasn't very appealing. The newly married men had young wives who loved them and brought them fresh cooked food for their meal break.

I was new to this job, and HR sent me to the lobby. A few young wives smiled and held containers of hot, steaming food: rice, meat, vegetables. Often when breaking the daily fast, it was a tradition to eat special food. I compare it to Christmas. If it was Christmastime, I'd enjoy Christmas cookies, our family's traditional soups, all the flavors and recipes of the holiday that we only eat at that time.

I got to the lobby, and there were a handful of women. A few more came, then more, and the far end of the lobby filled with young women bearing hearty food. Meal break came, and the husbands came over the stairs, then paused. I was suddenly pulled back to the memory of a junior high dance. Girls stood on one side, boys stood on the other. This was feeling stressful too, just like that junior high dance. The only thing missing was a DJ and a couple dance sponsors. Then it happened, just like at the dances. The first husband came forward, accepted his wife's delicious gift, and the awkward spell was broken. Everyone celebrated!

* * *

We hear a lot of speeches about compliance and safety. Well, meet the cow who was noncompliant. I'm not sure how it happened, but the story goes that a cow took things into his own hooves (hands) and headed for the hills. He got loose from the snaking line of cows, through a couple gates, and eventually strutted down the highway, intending to go home. Cars swerved to miss him. He was not going to be easily swayed by honks, hand gestures, or yelling. Eventually he was corralled, and back in line he went, but the story lives on! Cow escapes! Freedom for an hour! When his girlfriend told him, "I've had it. Hit the highway, Jack," he took it literally.

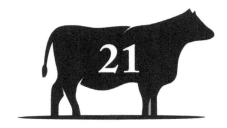

# Lead a Horse to Water

The most difficult part of chaplaincy (and many jobs that deal with helping people) is the person's right to choose.

Judy had a boyfriend for a dozen years. They lived together, and she envisioned them growing old together. They were intertwined in each other's families. Duke had a long list of disappointments and poor decisions. Judy had forgiven him over and over. "Why does he do these things?" Judy asked me.

I didn't have an answer. She wasn't even asking the right question, in my opinion. I thought she should kick him to the curb and never look back. One day he moved out. Now she had to decide whether to wait for him to return (which she'd done before) or move on without him. What I wanted didn't matter. It was her life and her decision. She moved on, and while the pain is still real and the heartache long-suffering, I support her in her new life, new choices, and the good she is pursuing. I know she wrestled with that decision.

"Chaplain Heidi," said a supervisor, "I've got a young woman I want you to talk to. She showed up with bruises today, and it's not the first time."

The supervisor asked her to come see me. He didn't tell her why she was coming, only that I wanted to see her. (Thanks, supervisor.)

I started out slowly, asking how things were going. We got down to the real problem. "But he loves me," she told me. She didn't want to talk to anyone—no counselor or support groups. She didn't want help from agencies. She didn't see this as a problem. They had two children together, I soon found out. "I've had both my kids with the same dad," she told me with great pride. Oh, if this was just a game of points, she might score a point for that, but there were some bigger issues. Their children had been taken away from the mother by child protective services. For a time, the children lived with a family member of the mother, and the mother was trying to get custody again. As long as she spent any time with the babies' daddy though, child protective services was clear the answer was no. The court case continued to drag along. The family member keeping the children told the mother if she continued with the boyfriend, this family member wouldn't keep her children, but put them in the foster care system. That scared the mother a bit, but she still wanted him in her life, and she dreamt of a future intact family, perfect and whole.

You know the saying "You can lead a horse to water, but you can't make them drink." I had an opinion, but ultimately, it wasn't my choice to make. I wasn't demanding. I did ask many questions though.

"So if you see your boyfriend, you'll lose your kids, right?"

"What did the social worker say? How far away could your children be if they put your children in foster care? That far? So you'd have to travel every weekend to see them? That would be a lot of energy, time, and money. What if you work six days a week? Would you have to miss that visit?"

They aren't my children. It's not my life. I am there to listen and help, to ask questions and try to make sure someone has seen many sides of the predicament. Ultimately, I'm not the one making the decision. These situations never have a quick, happy, Disney-like ending. I'll probably be the one she comes to talk to when her children are taken to a foster home farther away. She'll come to tell me how awful the system is, how awful her family is, and every other week, her boyfriend will be an angel or a devil.

Chaplains are there for the long roads, and sometimes even at the coolest creek after the arduous trek of life…the horse doesn't drink.

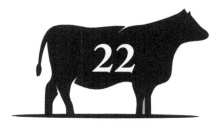

# My God, Your God

Are you a chaplain for *them* too?

You mean all the other religions besides Christianity and those who choose no religion? Why, yes, I am.

I drove a Somali woman to a doctor's appointment about two hours away. She didn't drive and didn't have transportation to see a specialist. She spoke English every day with her children, so we could talk. We chatted about our kids, work, favorite foods, all the things people getting to know each other talk about. She asked why Americans let animals live in their houses. She asked me why I (and most Americans) didn't care for rice very much, so I explained potatoes are the American equivalent of rice.

We returned to her house. I pulled up and stopped the car. She looked at me from the passenger side of the car, and her left eye peeked out from under her long head scarf. She got very quiet. She was almost whispering. "I think your god and my god are pretty close," she said.

That's my number one single best compliment I've ever received. It still makes me tear up. When I get too full of myself, I try to remember that I want people to see the Jesus living in me and through me.

Don't get me wrong. I can talk about Jesus all day long. He's my Savior. While it would be my wish that everyone knew Jesus as Savior and Lord, that's not my priority as a chaplain.

Someone gave me this analogy for those who work in ministry. During training (such as seminary), one is the fish in a fishbowl. Then when the person becomes a pastor, they are a fish in a pond or a lake. When a person works in a location such as a meat-packing plant, they become a fish in the ocean.

When people come for help, they have a specific need: finances, relationship, family, etc. They delay coming because it's personal, revealing, and sometimes embarrassing. I've got several goals:

1. Listen. I want to hear what they are saying and determine what their real need is.
2. Trust. I want them to trust me. I know trust is only beginning as we talk. They are waiting to see what happens, if I tell anyone, and most importantly, how I react to them.
3. Respect. Everyone deserves respect. Whatever the problem, it may seem small or inconsequential to the world, but to this person, it's taking over their life. I don't want to talk down to them, treat them like they don't matter, dismiss them out of hand, or reject them.
4. Mirror back to the person. "So what I'm hearing you say is…"

One of my favorite jokes: A farmer (let's say he's from Nebraska) decides he needs to diversify his business. Let's just say the blades on his combine aren't very sharp, if you know what I mean. He has been raising corn for years, and he decides he's going to raise chickens, too. He orders his first chicks. They arrive, and he dutifully plants them feet first in the ground, irrigates, and leaves. The chicks wriggle around, then die. Not easily swayed, the farmer orders a second batch.

They arrive. He plants these head first. The chicks put up a bigger fight at the beginning, but they too die. The poor farmer is beside himself. He calls the Nebraska Agriculture University and explains his predicament. The university answers, "Send soil samples."

As a chaplain, I have to be careful I'm not assuming too much. It's harder than you think not to assume. Even when I tell myself I have to be ready, to try and throw out all preconceived notions, they are the foundation of who I am. It takes work. Most people think this is what they're going to get from a chaplain:

1.  Recruit for Jesus. I'm going to arm wrestle you until you accept Jesus as your Lord and Savior and conform to my flavor of faith. (Flavor of faith is my go-to analogy. All faith is ice cream, just different flavors.)
2.  Chapter and verse. We'll create a Scripture list much like a music mix list that explains how to deal with your situation biblically. I'm going to spit it out at you, and everything will become crystal clear (and if not, just keep repeating until it becomes clear).
3.  Church-alyze. The person explains their church experience, or lack of experience, or lack of participation. There's an assumption all those of faith attend their house of worship (church, mosque, temple) regularly, and if they don't, they are unworthy, losers, undedicated. Yes, it's helpful to know the spiritual background of people, but there's no judgment. I've met church-hoppers, dyed-in-the wool loyalists, Chreasters (Christmas and Easter churchgoers), and everything else. People are sure that as a chaplain, I'm deducting points on their spiritual report card, but I'm not. Church is the first place I suggest people go when they need friends or when they feel lonely/abandoned/depressed. I'm very specific though. Don't slide into the back pew just as the service starts and flee from the back when it's over. People (especially women) need relationship. Join a Sunday school class,

a Bible study, a small group of some kind. If that doesn't work for you, join a bowling league, a knitting group, a book club. Everyone needs friends, real conversation, and more than a "like" on an app.

It's difficult to explain quickly and succinctly what a chaplain is and what they do, but I'm hoping this helps, and my number one hope for you is that you, too, receive a life-giving compliment that builds you up and pushes you forward in your faith.

"I think your god and my god are pretty close."

# Church studies inspire inmates

Chaplain Heidi and her mother featured in the
North Platte Telegraph Newspaper highlighting
their jail ministry in Dawson County jail.

Chaplain Heidi (left) helps distribute frozen chicken for employee appreciation and to assist during the Covid-19 pandemic.

Tyson employees, including Chaplain Heidi (left) show off their company's product as they assist at weekly local mobile food pantry distribution. People drive through this food pantry and volunteers load it in their trunks and they drive on-very Covid-19 friendly.

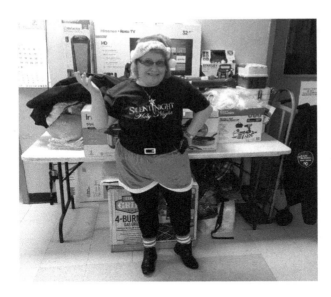

Celebrating Christmas at the plant is
Santa Helper Chaplain Heidi!

It's a s-p-o-o-k-y Halloween and nothings
makes people smile like a great costume!

The church the Revelos go to enjoys a Christmas Caroling Hayrack Ride. Sitting on haybales and riding around in the snow covered in blankets has become a church tradition. Chaplain Heidi's husband played the guitar as everyone sang.

Marco and Chaplain Heidi's two daughters.

# Vacuna Covida

*Sing to the tune of Akuna Matata

**Vacuna Covida**
**What a wonderful shot**
**Vacuna Covida**
**Doesn't take a lot**
**It means no worries**
**For the rest of your days**
**Vacuna Covida is**
**a problem-free**
**philosophy!**

**Vacuna Covida Ahorra!**

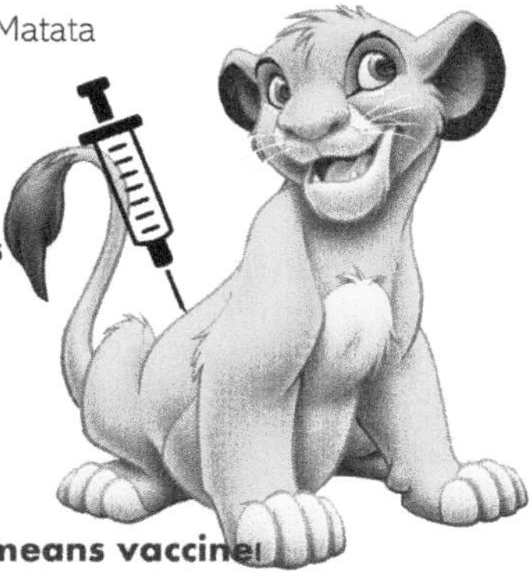

**\*Vacuna (Vah-koon-uh) means vaccine!**
**Go ahead, sing it again!**

Chaplain Heidi has a lot of creative energy. She
wrote this Covid-19 Vaccine parody song for fun
and people were humming the tune for days.

I am a chaplain.
I see things.
I hear things.
I know things.
If you could know what I know.
If you could feel what I feel.
If you could hear what I hear.
You would understand.
The man you see, looking strong, has just lost his father.
The woman you pass without a thought has been beaten.
The young worker who is limping as he smiles at you was shot in the ankle while running from his village.
The team member you see eating alone watched his sister get raped and shot.
That nice guy at your table was a child soldier.
The supervisor you are angry at is fighting depression.
The person speaking a different language wants so badly to know English, but finds it hard to do.
The tired man in the cafeteria sleeps in his car at night.
The middle-aged guy in your department lost custody of his kids.
The new hire has no food.
That young man sleeps on a hard floor each night in an empty apartment.
The woman in the line misses her baby at home, but needs money for rent.
The administrator doubts his decisions.
The guy you eat with is an alcoholic.
The young woman across the way is raising her kids alone.
Your coworker has a son in prison.
That guy with a sense of humor loses his money gambling each weekend.
That person who always seems heartless has had her heart ripped out by another.
That woman who tells you to move from her seat in the cafeteria cannot deal well with change.

The young worker doesn't have money for college.

That quiet guy has no friends, but desperately wants some.

The chaplain doesn't always smile, because sometimes things get to him.

We are normal, too.

All of us, everyone, has a story, a past.

Sometimes it is not pretty.

Love one another, treat each with respect, be kind because the world needs understanding.

There is enough pain already in everyone.

All these things I have seen.

I am a chaplain.


Chaplain Alan Cummins

CPSIA information can be obtained
at www.ICGtesting.com
Printed in the USA
LVHW070921180721
692992LV00024B/312